Rachel Carson
and Her Book That Changed the World

by Laurie Lawlor

illustrated by Laura Beingessner

Holiday House / New York

For my grandson
Beau Thomas Lawlor
—L. L.

For my mother, Sandra
—L. B.

Text copyright © 2012 by Laurie Lawlor
Illustrations copyright © 2012 by Laura Beingessner
All Rights Reserved
HOLIDAY HOUSE is registered in the U.S. Patent and Trademark Office.
Printed and Bound in March 2013 at Kwong Fat Offset Printing Co., Ltd.,
Dongguan City, China.
The text typeface is Hightower.
The illustrations were rendered in tempera paint and ink on paper.
www.holidayhouse.com

3 5 7 9 10 8 6 4 2

Library of Congress Cataloging-in-Publication Data
Lawlor, Laurie.
Rachel Carson and her book that changed the world / by Laurie Lawlor ; illustrations by Laura Beingessner.
p. cm.
ISBN 978-0-8234-2370-5 (hardcover)
1. Carson, Rachel, 1907–1964—Juvenile literature.
2. Biologists—United States—Biography—Juvenile literature.
3. Environmentalists—United States—Biography—Juvenile literature.
4. Carson, Rachel, 1907–1964. Silent spring.
I. Beingessner, Laura, 1965– ill. II. Title.
QH31.C33L39 2012 570.92—dc22
[B]
2010047302

ᴇARLY ONE MORNING in May 1922,
young Rachel Carson discovered a secret place
deep in the woods fragrant with pine needles.
"Witchity-witchity-witchity!"
called a yellowthroat.
Rachel followed the chanting wild bird
up and down the hills along the Allegheny River,
not stopping until she came upon its nest hidden in a bush.
Closer, closer she crept.
Click!
Her camera captured four eggs mottled white and brown,
precious as shining fruit.

3

All her life, Rachel Carson was curious and determined.
She was born on May 27, 1907, on the outskirts of Springdale,
a small town in Pennsylvania.
Since her brother and sister were much older
and neighborhood children seldom came to visit,
Rachel often went on her own to explore
her family's sixty-five acres of woods, orchards, and fields.

Her doting mother also loved nature.
She taught Rachel to skywatch on starry nights
and how to recognize the haunting melody of a wood thrush.
Rachel read constantly and worked hard in school.
When she was only eleven, her story about a brave pilot
won a prize and was published in *St. Nicholas Magazine* for children.
She decided to become a writer.

Times were tough. Rachel's father struggled to make a living
as a traveling salesman. Her fiercely proud mother
doubled her number of piano students
and sold apples, chickens—even the family china—
to help send Rachel to Pennsylvania College for Women
(later named Chatham College) in Pittsburgh.
Academic scholarship in hand, Rachel climbed
into a borrowed Model T and said good-bye.

College was a new world for shy Rachel.
While she enjoyed her writing classes,
she felt awkward at parties and dances.
When everyone else dressed up
to go to a concert at Carnegie Music Hall,
Rachel slipped away to study stuffed birds
at the nearby natural history museum.
Social life did not improve when Rachel's stern-faced mother
appeared on campus nearly every weekend to type Rachel's papers.

The summer when Rachel came home
after her first year at college,
a putrid smell lingered everywhere. Smoke clouded the sky.
Pollution floated on the river.
The woods were being cut down for factories and houses.
Too many quarreling people crowded her family's cramped house:
her parents, her poverty-stricken brother
and his wife and yowling baby,
her divorced sister and her two mischievous toddlers.
Even with a tent pitched in the front yard,
there was scarcely room for everyone.
Where could Rachel escape?
All this filled her with sadness and worries
about the environment and her own future.

When she returned to college, a biology class
taught by lively Miss Mary Scott Skinker changed her life.
At a time when few women pursued careers in science,
Rachel made up her mind to become a biologist.
There was so much she wanted to learn about animals and plants.
She knew she could find a way to pay for graduate school.
Sure enough, she won a full scholarship to Johns Hopkins University.

The summer before she started graduate school,
twenty-two-year-old Rachel traveled to Woods Hole, Massachusetts,
to study at a marine biology lab.
When she stood beside the Atlantic Ocean for the first time,
she lost her heart to a world of restless water and sky.
Surf crashed. Seabirds called. A briny smell filled the air.
Mysterious creatures scuttled in tide pools.
And what life hid deep below the ocean waves?

She received her master's degree—
one of only a handful of women in her class.
The Great Depression, a time of massive unemployment,
dashed her hope of continuing her studies.
No one wanted to hire a woman biologist.

When her father died, twenty-eight-year-old Rachel
was desperate for money to support her family.
Her mother, ailing sister, and two young nieces
lived elbow to elbow in Rachel's Maryland house.
Part-time jobs teaching and writing newspaper articles
barely paid the rent and grocery bills.
Rachel reached out to her former teacher.
Take the government scientist test, Miss Skinker suggested.
Rachel aced the exam but still had no job offers.
She did not give up. She kept knocking on doors and sending letters.

Mary Scott Skinker

One day the chief of the Bureau of Fisheries interviewed Rachel.

Sorry, no jobs, he told her. Maybe she'd be interested in trying to fix

dull radio scripts about sea life?

Every other writer had tried and failed.

"I've never seen a word of yours," she later remembered him saying,

"but I'm going to take a sporting chance."

This was Rachel's lucky break.

Her scripts were a success.

She landed a full-time job as a biologist at the Bureau of Fisheries,

one of only two professional women on the staff.

When she was assigned to write about the sea for a radio broadcast,

the material, she said, "rather took charge of the situation."

Her boss read her lengthy work and handed it back to her

with a twinkle in his eye.

"I don't think it will do. Better try again.

But send this one to *The Atlantic*."

She followed his advice.

When the magazine printed "Undersea,"

Rachel was approached by an editor from a book publisher.

Why not write about the sea for ordinary readers?

In 1941 she published her first book,

Under the Sea-Wind: A Naturalist's Picture of Ocean Life,

just as Pearl Harbor in Hawaii was bombed

and America began its involvement in World War II.

The book—mostly unnoticed

—quickly disappeared from bookstore shelves.

Rachel did not stop researching and writing
about the remarkable connections in the web of life.
"Once you are *aware* of the wonder and beauty of earth,"
she scribbled in her journal,
"you will want to learn about it."

As a biologist for fifteen years,
she went places where few women ventured.
She did work performed by few women:
counting deep-sea fish in foggy,
dangerous currents south of Nova Scotia;
observing reef animals in a special suit
with an eighty-four-pound diving helmet
off the coast of Florida;
tracking alligators atop a rumbling "glades buggy"
in the swampy Florida Everglades.

Meanwhile she worked on her own writing in the evening or on weekends.

She began to notice disturbing trends.

What happened to the web of life

when more and more garbage was dumped into the ocean?

How did rising ocean temperatures affect living creatures?

In 1951 she published a best seller, *The Sea Around Us*.

A year later she quit her job to write full-time.

During the next three years, she researched and wrote

The Edge of the Sea.

She was so well-known that people demanded her autograph

in elevators, beauty parlors, taxicabs, and restaurants.

Rachel never married.
Not only was she the sole breadwinner, she was also responsible
for the care of many different family members
when they were unemployed, ill, or dying.
At age fifty she adopted her niece's five-year-old son, Roger.
Now she faced the challenge of taking care of a wild young boy
and finding time to write.

As always, the outdoors was her refuge.

She bought a few acres of land along her beloved Maine coast

and built a summer cottage.

"A treasure of a place," she called it.

By day she enjoyed wandering with Roger

to inspect moss and ferns among the deep, dark trees.

At night during low tide she took a flashlight

and went alone to the rocky shore.

She rolled up the legs of her pants and wriggled on her stomach,

discovering big scurrying crabs, starfish, and anemones.

In 1958 she began a difficult new project.

When World War II ended, the chemical industry
in the United States had become very powerful.

Heavy spraying of chemicals to kill insects was done routinely
in parks and nature preserves—even in swimming pools
and on crowded city streets.

As early as 1945, Rachel had read about studies
of declining bird populations across the country.

Each year researchers reported fewer nesting and migrating birds.

The more she investigated, the more alarmed she became.

Insecticides were deadly to birds, insects, fish, and other animals.

What about people?

No one had taken a stand against big business,
federal agencies that approved chemical use,
or universities that performed shoddy research
about the effects of chemicals.

She knew she was walking into dangerous territory.

However, because she had no connection with industry,
government, or any university,
she felt she could gather facts more freely.

People would read what she wrote and fight
to demand clean air, clean water.

Only Rachel's closest friends knew she was in a race against time.
In 1960 she was diagnosed with breast cancer.
Her book *Silent Spring* was something she believed in so deeply,
"nothing . . . made me ever consider turning back."
She worked for four years to complete *Silent Spring*.
Her careful research about insecticides was slow.
Her writing and rewriting was even slower.
She wanted to create a book
that everyone—not just scientists—could understand.

In spite of being bedridden with illness and exhaustion,
she refused to give up.
"I could never again listen happily to a thrush song," she explained,
"if I had not done all I could."

In 1962 *Silent Spring* was published
and became a best seller.
The book created a firestorm of criticism
from the chemical industry.
Congress held hearings.
Investigations followed.
New laws were written.
Rachel did not live to see
the many positive environmental changes
created by so many ordinary people
inspired by her brave book.
On April 14, 1964,
just before an early spring sunset
filled with birdsong,
fifty-six-year-old Rachel died.

The author of THE SEA AROUND US and
THE EDGE OF THE SEA
questions our attempt to control the
natural world around us

SILENT
SPRING
Rachel
Carson

Epilogue

WHAT HAPPENED AFTER THE PUBLICATION OF *SILENT SPRING*

Silent Spring's powerful title came from the image of a spring gone silent of songbirds. *The New Yorker* printed advance excerpts of *Silent Spring* beginning on June 16, 1962. Houghton Mifflin published the book on September 27. Almost immediately, a major chemical company threatened to sue *The New Yorker* and Houghton Mifflin to stop publication. Neither the magazine nor the book publisher backed down. A full-blown chemical industry attack erupted. *Silent Spring* became an immediate best seller.

The chemical industry and several government agencies mounted a vicious, well-funded campaign against *Silent Spring* and Carson, who was called "an hysterical woman" who was "probably a Communist." A former secretary of agriculture wrote to President Dwight D. Eisenhower and asked "why a spinster with no children was so concerned about genetics." One critic called her book "emotional and alarmist" and labeled Carson part of a noisy, misinformed group of "organic-gardening faddists and other beyond-the-fringe groups."

Ultimately, Carson was vindicated.

Public outcry created an avalanche of letters to Congress, the Departments of Agriculture and the Interior, the Public Health Service, and the Food and Drug Administration. Newspapers and magazines ran scathing editorials and letters to the editor. In August 1962, President John F. Kennedy assigned a special panel of the President's Science Advisory Committee to investigate insecticide use. Their published report criticized the chemical industry and government agencies. Carson presented her warnings directly to television audiences with a special interview on *CBS Reports* in April 1963. A Senate committee on environmental hazards televised Carson's urgent testimony two months later.

Meanwhile, *Silent Spring* became a best seller in Great Britain and was published in France, Germany, Italy, Denmark, Sweden, Norway, Holland, Spain, Brazil, Japan, Iceland, Portugal, and Israel. Honors and awards poured in. In March 1963 she was named Conservationist of the Year by the National Wildlife Federation. She received the conservation award from the Isaak Walton League of America, the Audubon Medal from the National Audubon Society, and the Cullum Medal from the American Geographical Society. She was one of only four women elected to the American Academy of Arts and Letters.

Much remains to be done to combat serious on-going environmental threats. At the same time, it's important to keep in mind how truth eloquently expressed continues to have the power to change the world. The years following the publication of *Silent Spring* inspired grassroot environmental groups and other local citizens to push for the passage of federal laws protecting the environment.

After long battles in court, widespread use of DDT was banned in 1972. Thanks to Carson's groundwork, continuing research proved that DDT has disastrous effects on healthy bird reproduction.

Silent Spring not only saved many bird species; it also opened the minds of millions to what was considered to be a new concept at the time: what we do to the air, water, and soil directly affects us, future generations, and animals and plants that share the earth with us. Rachel Carson demonstrated how one committed person can make a difference. As former Vice President Al Gore, who currently works on issues of global warming, said, "*Silent Spring* came as a cry in the wilderness, a deeply felt, thoroughly researched, and brilliantly written argument that changed the course of history. Without this book, the environmental movement might have been long delayed or never have developed at all."

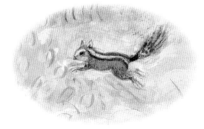

SOURCE NOTES

Look for more resources at www.holidayhouse.com

PAGE 3: "Rachel followed . . . shining fruit." Carson wrote about this experience in "My Favorite Recreation," a story she wrote for *St. Nicholas Magazine* (July 1922): 999.

PAGE 5: "When she was . . . writer." Rachel sent off her first story, "A Battle in the Clouds," to the *St. Nicholas* League Contest in May 1918. When the September 1918 issue arrived, she discovered her published story and her silver badge award. Eagerly, she sent off four more stories, all published in 1919. She later said, "I can remember no time, even in earliest childhood, when I didn't assume I was going to be a writer." Her early writing experience is described in *Rachel Carson: Witness for Nature*, pp. 18–19. Her quote comes from "The Real World Around Us," a speech given at the Theta Sigma Phi Matrix Table Dinner, April 21, 1954, Columbus, Ohio. Rachel Carson Papers, Yale Collection of American Literature, Beinecke Rare Book and Manuscript Library, Yale University, New Haven, Connecticut. See also *Lost Woods*, pp. 148–163, for the full speech transcript.

PAGE 6: "When everyone . . . museum." Anecdote about her avoiding social functions to go to a museum appears in Wendy Wareham's "Rachel Carson's Early Years," *Carnegie Magazine*, 58, no. 6 (November 1986).

PAGE 6: "Social life . . . papers." Stories about Rachel's mother on campus were gathered together from interviews with Rachel's fellow students in *Rachel Carson: Witness for Nature*, pp. 30–31.

PAGE 10: "When she stood . . . ocean waves?" Carson described her experience beside the sea in the speech "The Real World Around Us." Exact citation appears in *Lost Woods*, pp. 148–9.

PAGE 14: "I've never . . . chance." Carson recalled her experience and her boss's comments in her speech "The Real World Around Us." Rachel Carson Papers.

PAGE 14: "When she was assigned . . . *Atlantic*." Carson recalled her work and his suggestion in her speech "The Real World Around Us." Rachel Carson Papers.

PAGE 17: "Once you . . . it." Carson wrote this note to herself while writing "Help Your Child To Wonder." Rachel Carson Papers. The article eventually appeared in *Woman's Home Companion* 83 (July 1956): 25–27, 46–48.

PAGE 18: "glades buggy." Carson's speech "The Real World Around Us." Rachel Carson Papers.

PAGE 20: "She began to . . . living creatures?" Carson constantly compiled research and investigated studies about the sea. Some of this material appeared in a paper presented at the American Association for the Advancement of Science Symposium, "The Sea Frontier." She presented this paper December 29, 1953, Boston, Massachusetts. Rachel Carson Papers. The text about global/sea warming appears in *Lost Woods*, p. 135.

PAGE 24: "It is a treasure of a place to which I have lost my heart, completely." Carson wrote of the forest, shoreline, and small beach area in a letter to Curtis and Nellie Lee Bok, December 12, 1956. Rachel Carson Papers. Exact quote appears in *Lost Woods*, p. 174.

PAGE 24: "At night . . . anemones." She wrote of her adventures in Maine in a letter to her agent, Marie Rodell, August, 28, 1953.

Rachel Carson Papers.

PAGE 26: "No one . . . freely." In February 1959, Carson sent a letter to *The New Yorker* editor William Shawn and Paul Brooks of Houghton Mifflin outlining her plan to "achieve . . . a synthesis of widely scattered facts, that have not heretofore been considered in relation to each other. It is now possible to build up, step by step, a really damning case against the use of these chemicals as they are now inflicted upon us." *Rachel Carson: Witness for Nature*, 340. Carson and Brooks exchanged a number of letters in March 1960 in which she described her plan and how she would list her principle sources, including technical journals, in an appendix arranged by chapter as an alternative to footnotes. *Rachel Carson: Witness for Nature*, 366. Carson said, "Doing this will, I think, serve a double purpose: It will make the book more useful to the serious student, and it will refute any claims that my views are personal and ill-founded." Letter to Paul Brooks, March 23, 1960. Rachel Carson Papers.

PAGE 26: "People . . . clean water." Carson wrote about giving people "the facts they need to fight with" in a letter to Dorothy Freeman, January 6, 1962. *Always, Rachel*, 391.

PAGE 28: "nothing . . . back." Carson recorded her feelings in a letter to Dorothy Freeman, June 27, 1962. *Always, Rachel*, 408.

PAGE 28: "I could . . . could." Rachel wrote this comment in a letter to Dorothy Freeman, January 23, 1963. *Always, Rachel*, 394.

PAGE 31: "an hysterical woman," "probably a Communist," and "why a . . . genetics." *Rachel Carson: Witness for Nature*, 429–30, footnote 4, p. 573.

PAGE 31: "emotional and alarmist" and "organic-gardening faddists . . . groups." Edwin Diamond, "The Myth of the 'Pesticide Menace,'" *Saturday Evening Post* 236 (28 September 1963). *DDT, Silent Spring, and the Rise of Environmentalism*, 115.

PAGE 31: "Silent Spring . . . all." Al Gore, "Rachel Carson and *Silent Spring*," in *Courage for the Earth*, 63–64.

SOURCES AND RECOMMENDED READING

BOOKS BY RACHEL CARSON

1941. *Under the Sea-Wind: A Naturalist's Picture of Ocean Life*. New York: Simon & Schuster.

1951. *The Sea Around Us*. New York: Oxford University Press.

1955. *The Edge of the Sea*. Boston: Houghton Mifflin.

1961. *The Sea Around Us*. Rev. Ed. New York: Oxford University Press.

1962. *Silent Spring*. Boston: Houghton Mifflin.

1965. *The Sense of Wonder*. New York and Evanston: Harper & Row.

BOOKS ABOUT RACHEL CARSON

Dunlap, Thomas R., ed. *DDT, Silent Spring, and the Rise of Environmentalism*. Seattle: University of Washington Press, 2008.

Freeman, Martha, ed. *Always, Rachel: The Letters of Rachel Carson and Dorothy Freeman, 1952–1964*. Boston: Beacon Press, 1995.

Lear, Linda. *Rachel Carson: Witness for Nature*. New York: Holt, 1997.

———. *Lost Woods: The Discovered Writing of Rachel Carson*. Boston: Beacon Press, 1980.

Matthiessen, Peter, ed. *Courage for the Earth: Writers, Scientists, and Activists Celebrate the Life and Writing of Rachel Carson*. Boston: Houghton Mifflin, 2007.